Cambellism

by

W.B. Godbey

First Fruits Press
Wilmore,
Kentucky
c2018

Campbellism by W.B. Godbey

Published by First Fruits Press, © 2018
Previously Published

ISBN: 9781621718369 (print), 9781621718376 (digital), 9781621718383 (kindle)

Digital version at http://place.asburyseminary.edu/godbey/22/

For all other uses, contact:

First Fruits Press
B.L. Fisher Library
Asbury Theological Seminary
204 N. Lexington Ave.
Wilmore, KY 40390
http://place.asburyseminary.edu/firstfruits

Godbey, W. B. (William Baxter), 1833-1920.

Campbellism / by W.B. Godbey.
Wilmore, KY : First Fruits Press, ©2018.
31 p. ; cm.
Reprint. Previously published: [Place of publication not identified] : [publisher not identified], [190-?]
ISBN: 9781621718369 (pbk.)
1. Disciples of Christ--Controversial literature. I. Title.

BX7323.G62 2018   286.6

Cover design by Jon Ramsay

asburyseminary.edu
800.2ASBURY
204 North Lexington Avenue
Wilmore, Kentucky 40390

First Fruits
THE ACADEMIC OPEN PRESS OF ASBURY SEMINARY

First Fruits Press
The Academic Open Press of Asbury Theological Seminary
204 N. Lexington Ave., Wilmore, KY 40390
859-858-2236
first.fruits@asburyseminary.edu
asbury.to/firstfruits

CAMPBELLISM

by

W. B. GODBEY

In this writing I am frank to confess that I am close to home, as I was born and reared in the hot-bed of Campbellism, and the first twenty years of my life, until I bade my native land adieu for the prosecution of my collegiate education (which was an absolute necessity, as there were no colleges in all that region of country in 1853), I heard them preach five times as much as all other denominations.

When I was a little boy, Alexander Campbell, the founder of this church, came into that country, and produced a great sensation and received a host of followers. In those days he and Barton Stone, the founder of the Newlight Church, were comrade evangelists; the former originally a Baptist and the latter a Presbyterian; both having received a splendid education and good experiences of the blessed supernatural birth wrought in the heart by the Holy Spirit. Campbell certified with his trenchant pen (I have read his books much to my edification), that an experience which is not begun, perpetuated and consummated in the heart by the Holy Spirit is utterly inadequate to insure admission into Heaven. This was in his early writings. In subsequent years, his writings and his

1

preaching show plainly his mournful apostasy from his spiritual experience and lamentable drift not only into heresy, appertaining to the work of the Spirit, but even into idolatry, appertaining to water baptism, making immersion in water essential to salvation; thus running into gross idolatry; as you might just as well worship a god of wood or stone as water.

When he drifted into heresy on the Holy Ghost and idolatry on water baptism, Barton Stone dissented from him, debated with him, and did his best to re-claim him, but signally failed; consequently, they both founded churches, Campbell calling his "The Disciples," and Stone his, "The Christian Newlights." The latter received a following, but only a handful comparatively with the thronging multitudes who followed the former, who after awhile changed their name to "Christian," for which they are everywhere quite stickleristic in contradistinction to "Campbellite," which they reject with indignation; but I use it in a theological sense, as it is the only cognomen available which is free from ambiguity. As to the term "Christian," six hundred millions are thus designated, and with the exception of a few locations on the earth, no auditor or reader would even have an idea that I meant the church about which I am now writing. I use the term "Campbellite" with the greatest respect, as they are my old neighbors and friends, whom I dearly love. Therefore, I write this booklet in perfect love for those people, and unhesitatingly say that if God needs a martyr to save them from the awful soul-destroying heresies in which the enemy has caught them, I put in the first bid. They are the preachers of my childhood, striplinghood and youth, and my beloved companions in life's morning. I never can forget them. I am now in my eightieth year. How I would be delighted to lay down my life and go up to Heaven with the martyr's crown shining on my brow, if, in so doing, I could save those people. I can certainly say like Paul in behalf of his people (Rom. 9th chap.), "Would that I were a sacrifice from Christ, for the sake of my brethren, the comrades of my childhood!"

The Lord has so wonderfully saved me, that I can never be anything but His mouthpiece. Such you will find me in this and all of my writings.

(a) Very recently it was my privilege to preach in a Newlight church in Indiana. I found them biblically orthodox on the grand essentials of salvation, the supernatural birth for every sinner, and entire sanctification for every Christian; enjoying the shine, the shout and leap, living in the glorious anticipation of the Lord's return to the earth to reign in righteousness, and shouting at the thought of hearing Him call His bride, and the archangel sound his trumpet.

The situation reminded me of the ministry of Barton Stone, who separated from Campbell when he went back on Holy Ghost religion and drifted away into that wild fanaticism appertaining to water baptism. How do you account for the fact that Stone has so few followers and Campbell so many? Jesus answers the question (Matt. 7:13):

"Broad is the road that leads to death,
And thousands walk together there;
While wisdom shows a narrow path,
With here and there a traveler."

(*b*) So long as Satan is on the throne of the world, the saved will be "only here and there a traveler;" while the multitudes will throng the broad road that leads to death. Second Corinthians 4:4, which calls Satan "the god of this world," is the wrong translation; it should read, "the god of this age." It is exceedingly consolatory to know that he is not the God of this world, because it is felicitously included in the redemption, and Peter tells us all about its sanctification by fire, like your soul and mine, simultaneously with the final Judgment.

N. B. While the final Judgment is in progress (which will not be a twenty-four hour day, as is man's, but God's day, and He will take plenty of time), meanwhile this earth will be wrapped in her fiery sanctification, burning out not only all sin, but all the effects of sin, which had been wrought on her by sinners peregrinating all over her surface, through Satan's long, rolling ages, which began with the fall and will wind up with his arrest by the apocalyptic angel (Rev. 20:1-4), and ejectment into Hell. During Satan's age, he has the long end of the rope, the broad side of the battle-field, and the big run of things; thronging multitudes frolicking down the broad way; meanwhile the "King's Highway of Holiness" has "but here and there a traveler."

Our dispensation will never get the world saved; though the Gospel is perfectly free and all might be saved, yet Satan is so strongly influential that the saved will be only a few (Luke 13:23) in our dispensation.

Jesus Himself settles this matter (Luke 21st chap.) where He certifies that the world will get worse and worse till He comes suddenly, and illustrates it by the ante-diluvians who, despite the faithful preaching of Noah, 120 years without a flicker, rushed heedlessly on, from bad to worse, till the flood came and took them all away.

He also illustrates the same awful truth appertaining to our dispensation by Sodom and Gomorrah, which God destroyed for their wickedness, who, despite the preaching of Lot twenty-three years, rushed recklessly on, getting worse and worse till the angels took Lot and his wife and daughters by the hand and led them out (because he signally failed to prevail on his married daughters and sons-in-law to leave the city), and God rained fire and brimstone from Heaven and destroyed them all.

N. B. God's Word settles everything for time and eternity. Satan has filled the world with churches, in order to deceive the people and lead them into Hell by millions blindfolded, deceived and led astray by his counterfeit preachers, who still, as in former days, lull the people into a deeper sleep, crying out, "Peace, peace, when there is no peace."

(c) While formal churches superabound on all sides, competing with each other for numbers, instead of souls, Campbellism is peculiar in the fact that it is no fallen church; as Campbell, after he backslid and went into fanaticism and idolatry on immersion, founded it in 1823, down on Satan's bottom, whence there is no place into which to fall during probation till the end comes and his people all drop down into Hell, eternally sinking into a deeper and more dismal woe, as Hell has no bottom.

Frequently while crossing the great oceans, in the dead hours of the night, I have heard the stentorian shouts of the sounders, reporting the depth of the sea in their strange nautical language, till finally they roar out the loud acclaim, "No bottom!" meaning that they had reached water so deep that no lead and line could sound it; reminding me of the lugubrious wails of the damned, going up while the ages of eternity speed their precipitate flight, wailing on and on, "No bottom!"

As Satan is the god of this age, and so much wiser than any human being, and he started out as God's rival, claiming to be God, and has ever since been playing God on the people, therefore the great rank and file of nominal Christians are devil worshippers. They are not directly so, like multitudes in heathen lands, who offer sacrifices to him to appease his wrath and mitigate his punishment; *e. g.,* Israel from the days of Solomon to Josiah had the statue of Moloch (the devil) in the valley of Hinnom, in the shape of a man with the head of an ox, and would heat it hot by fire within and lay a child in its arms and make music so loudly that they could not hear it cry, till it utterly burnt up; thus worshipping the devil, to mitigate the punishment they feared he would inflict on them.

The Spiritualists all worship demons, which they claim to be the spirits of their departed relatives and friends; but which show plainly their hellish identity by frequently telling lies, which only Satan and his people can do. A great Spiritualist in Denver admitted that some were lying spirits.

As these demons are all fallen angels, and older than Adam and Eve would be if they were now living on the earth, they have much knowledge beyond the possibility of mortals. When they know that, as a rule it will suit their evil purposes to tell the truth, they do so, whereas they supply the vacuum of their own ignorance by falsification.

(d) The reason why the Tongues Movement is so detrimental to spirituality, causing the people to backslide so quickly, is because they go into demon worship like the Spiritualists, by having communion with the evil spirits, which would give them tongues, i. e., languages, if they could; but as they cannot, they give them noises like birds and frogs, in order to deceive them and get them away from God. It is a well-attested fact that what they call "tongues" is no tongue, but only noises, because a tongue is a language, and if they had it, somebody would understand it. This phenomenon came into the Holiness Movement from the Spiritualists. The Mormons have had it from the days of Joe Smith. The wizards, witches, sorcerers, jugglers, necromancers, enchanters, legerdemainers and magicians in all ages have had it. Satan and his myrmidons counterfeit everything God does. in order to deceive the people and get them away from God.

How can I fortify myself against the millions of demons who are sweeping through the air on all sides, led by Satan (Eph. 2:1)? If you will be true to God's triple leadership, you will be amply fortified against them, so they can never hurt you. Man is a trinity, consisting of spirit, soul and body. The human spirit consists of the conscience, the will and the affections. The soul is constituted of the animal life, the intellect, the memory, the judgment and the sensibilities, while your body is simply the tenement in which you live. The Holy Spirit leads our spirit; the Word, our mind, and God's providence leads our body. If we are true to this wonderful triple leadership of the Lord, we are as sure of Heaven as if we were in it, shouting round the throne. The devil cannot do anything with you but tempt you, so long as you are true to the triple leadership; meanwhile all the temptations he can possibly bring into availability, through the media of all his myrmidons, whose name is legion, God will make a blessing to your soul, if you are true to His triple leadership, having no leader but Jesus, no guide but the Holy Ghost, and no authority but the precious Word.

(e) While Satan directly, through his millions of myrmidons, is doing his utmost to sidetrack people and get them to follow him or some demon, who will lead them to Hell as certainly as Diabolus himself, the work he is doing indirectly, under the name of God, is magnitudinous, and alarming in the extreme. Oh, that the people would study and obey God's Word.

1 John 4:1: "Try the spirits and see if they are of

God; because many false prophets have gone out into the world."

Five hundred millions of Catholics and two hundred millions of Protestants all wear the Christian cognomen; Satan and his emissaries doing their best to get them to believe that they are Christians, so they will content themselves without salvation. Satan is so wise and smart that he always puts a good label on his goods, so as to allure, fascinate and satisfy the people. It is his glory to fill up Hell with people wearing the Christian name and every other good name. You need not think that Satan is fool enough to let his people wear a bad name, as in that case they would take alarm and leave him, slipping out of his fingers, getting away forever, and shouting the victory world without end.

Now suppose your name is "Christian," and you are not one, what is the conclusion? Why, you are a hypocrite and hastening to the hottest doom in Hell. What is a hypocrite? The word simply means one who plays religion, when he does not have it.

Campbellism is downright and unambuscaded hypocrisy, because they preach with all their might salvation by works, which is Satan's sleekest plank to Hell, as good works are so plausible that Satan can very successfully manipulate them into the fatal delusion and damnation of your soul.

I heard the Campbellites preach constantly for the first twenty years of my life; the greatest men of their kingdom, all sorts and sizes. They denied the personality of the Holy Ghost, which is downright infidelity; and made church-joining the great, salient point, as

they do this day. I travel more than any man you
ever saw, around the historic world four times, and
crossing this continent immemorially, preaching from
the Atlantic to the Pacific, and I strike them in my
peregrinations everywhere I go, especially in the West
and South. It is the same old thing which I heard and
saw those twenty years—join the church, confess the
Christhood of Jesus, get immersed in water for the re-
mission of sins, and take the name Christian—a hotch
potch of falsification and hypocrisy from beginning
to end, without a scintilla of salvation; thus deceiv-
ing the people and giving them a ticket to Heaven
through their church, denominated "Christian," while
it is simply Satan's passport to Hell—appalling in the
extreme.

(f) What about church-joining? It is Satan's
hoax to fool a poor sinner and dump him into Hell.
What is the Church? *Ecclesia*, from *ek*, out, and
kaleo, to call; so it means "the called-out people,"
i. e., the souls who have heard the call of the Holy
Ghost and come to God with a broken heart and a
contrite spirit, whom He gladly receives for Jesus'
sake, and freely pardons. Then the Holy Spirit raises
such a soul from the dead, creating in him a new heart
and a new spirit, which consummate the supernatural
birth, in which he is born into God's family, which is
the Church, and the only Church He has in all the
world.

The very idea that you can join the Church of God
is a heresy hatched in Hell and propagated by Satan
through his false prophets for the swift damnation
which is so rapidly filling up Hell. Our children are

not joined into our families, but born into them. So with the family of God, "ye must be born from above." (John 3:7.) Without this supernatural birth, there is no Christian and no Heaven. Oh, how Satan floods the world with his delusions, filling it up with hypocrites, utterly ignorant of the supernatural birth!

Jesus, in His preaching, in harmony with the whole Bible, consigns all sinners to Hell, and of all the lost souls in the world, He most terrifically anathematizes hypocrites, "O ye scribes and Pharisees, hypocrites, how can you escape the damnation of Hell!" He repeated these terrific anathemas over and over in His daily preaching, making them so awfully mad that they actually killed Him. These were the preachers, officers and leading people of the Church.

(g) Very few people know what a hypocrite is, The Greek word means a tragedian on the stage acting an unreal part, e. g., you go to the theater and are charmed by the Comanche Indian, whereas there was no Indian there, but the man was a painted citizen of Cincinnati, playing the part of a Comanche Indian.

It is distressing to know that the Campbellite Church is already large and growing faster than any other, because it has no cross on which to crucify old Adam, even, in its awful pelagian heresy, denying that you are born with inbred sin in the heart.

When I was preaching in San Francisco, Evangelist Martin, standing at the front of their church, responsively to a question ringing out to an audience, "What is inbred sin?" answered, "There is no such thing." So they make short work of it, by repudiating hereditary depravity and thus utterly sweeping sanctification from the field, as it means the purification of the heart from inbred sin, whereas, if there is none, there can be no sanctification. But what are you going to do with your Bible, where it says: "I was shapen in iniquity, and in sin did my mother conceive me" (Psa. 51:5), and, "Follow peace with all people, and the sanctification, without which no one shall see the Lord" (Heb. 12:14)?

N. B. God's Word will judge you in the great day, when the poor Campbellite preachers will be unable to help themselves, being in the same condemnation, much less to do anything for you. The reason I write this awful truth is because God will put me on the witness stand, and I do this that I may be "free from the blood of all men." The simple truth is, any and every person claiming to be a Christian, without the supernatural birth wrought in the heart by the Holy Ghost, is Satan's hypocrite, whom Jesus consigns to the most awful doom of the damned.

It is an indisputable fact that the Campbellite Church gives nobody any chance for salvation. God is so good that He saves everybody who will give Him a chance, regardless of religion, politics, nationality, race, color, or anything else incident to probationary life. His loving invitation is to all, and none of us has anything to do but to radically repent of all our sins, making confession and restitution, so far as possible, giving them all back to the devil, whence we got them, and bidding him an eternal adieu, go out of business with him in every form and phase, world without end. Then utterly and eternally abandon to God, spirit, soul and body.

"Here I give my all to Thee,
        Friends and time and earthly store,
Soul and body Thine to be,
        Wholly Thine forever more.

"Wash me in the Savior's precious blood,
        Cleanse me in the purifying flood,
        Here I give my life to Thee,
        Thine henceforth eternally."

(h) If Campbellism were true, that you can be saved by reformation (as Mr. Campbell gives it in his translation, instead of repentance), confession, immersion and keeping the commandments, then Jesus died for nothing. (Gal. 2: 21.) We had the commandments away back in Eden; we had as much water in the world (Noah's flood) before Christ came as we have ever had since. Therefore we could have kept the commandments and taken all the water we wanted, as well, if He had stayed in Heaven, as if He came into this world of sin and sorrow, suffered, bled and died to redeem us from sin, death and Hell.

This attitude toward the work of Christ is awfully wicked and blasphemous; having the poor, lost people come to the preacher (a poor sinner who can't save himself), instead of to Jesus, "mighty to save;" and to a human organization, instead of to the glorious Church of the First-born, which can only be entered by the supernatural birth; and to the water instead of to the Holy Ghost, thus running people into idolatry as gross as that of the Hindoo worshiping his stone god, and depending on his own obedience to save him instead of on the obedience of Christ.

Jesus took our place, perfectly obeyed the Divine law, thus becoming our substitute actively, keeping the law for us, and as we had all violated it, fallen under condemnation and come short of the glory of God, and were thus doomed to eternal damnation, He took our place under the law, suffered, bled and died to redeem us from sin, death and Hell, arose triumphantly over death, Hell and the grave, ascended on high, sitteth on the right hand of the Father, and maketh intercession for us lost sinners.

(*i*) This glorious, omnipotent Christ needs no help to save us, and when we bring in the preacher, water, our good works, or anything else to help Him, grieved and broken-hearted over our impenitence and unbelief, retreating away He leaves us to our idols, to "believe lies and be damned." (2 Thess. 2:12.) The Campbellite confession is simply a ridiculous farce, as no one can say Jesus is Lord but by the Holy Ghost. (1 Cor. 12:4.) You do not know that He is the Christ till you test Him, He saves you, and the Holy Spirit witnesses to you the fact that your sins are forgiven, you are born from above and your name is written in Heaven.

When Jesus was on the earth, the demons (who were fallen angels and had known Him in Heaven before they fell) confessed Him everywhere He went, but He hushed them all up, being unwilling to have their testimony. Sinners are incarnate demons and utterly unacquainted with Jesus, so their confession is a blasphemous farce. Why don't they get them down on their knees till they pray through and the Holy Ghost reveals Jesus to them as He did to Saul of Tarsus on the Damascus road, and to every other sinner who ever does get saved? Then they will confess Him with radiant faces and shouts of victory. What an awful pity to have poor, lost, ignorant men and women, exposed to wrath and Hell, thus hallucinated and humbugged by unconverted preachers and church-members calling themselves Christians, when aliens to God, strangers to grace, and exposed to wrath and Hell!

Misery loves company, consequently churches which have no salvation are the most aggressive and the most proselytic in all the world, e. g., the Jewish Church. It had degenerated into dead formality, hollow hypocrisy, and even gross idolatry, because they had idolized the Mosaic ordinances augmented by the traditions of the elders, and Jesus told them that they were compassing sea and land to make one proselyte, and when they had done their work he was two-fold more the child of Hell, i. e., to his own multitudinous iniquities he had added the awful sin of hypocrisy, being catalogued with the people of God when still a citizen of Satan's kingdom!

(j) Thus the Campbellite Church, under the enticing cognomen "Christian," is adroitly used by Satan to capture ignorant people, vainly hallucinated with the fond delusion that, if they become members of the "Christian (?) Church" they are Christians. This would be true if they did become members of the Christian Church, which they can only do by getting born from above (John 3: 7), in which case the Holy Ghost gives the new heart, and new spirit, actually creating the "new man," in the fallen soul and witnessing to His own mighty work so clearly that you will know it better than you know anything else, and the shine of Heaven on your face will make you the advertiser of your own salvation to everybody you meet. When God makes you a Christian, you know it so well that you really care nothing about what people call you. They have called God's people hard names in all ages; but they care nothing about it and wear the cognomen till heavenly lustre so accumulates on it that its primitive reproach goes into eclipse.

Campbellism actually gives you no chance for your life, because it is as destitute of the grand *sine qua nons* of experimental salvation as the farmer's almanac or the Koran of Mohammed. You can get saved in the Campbellite Church, Roman Catholic, Moslem or anywhere else. "In the day thou seekest me with all thy heart, I will be found of thee." God's Word can't fail. Therefore nobody has anything to do but seek Him with his whole heart and salvation comes along, a heavenly cyclone, giving him the shine, the shout, and the leap.

I preached one day last August in a Kentucky camp-meeting, led by a flaming Holiness evangelist, who told me in private conversation that he had been born, reared and educated in the Campbellite Church, thinking he was a Christian till, in the good providence of God, conviction opened his eyes to see himself a poor, lost sinner, an alien to God and a stranger to grace. Going off to a mountain alone, and falling down before God, he said, "Now, Jesus, I have come out here to get you to save my soul, and if you do not, somebody, some one, will come along here and find a pile of bones." You know Jesus never lets a case of that kind go by. The result was, he left the mountain ere long a new creature, with the whole world looking new, bright and beautiful on all sides.

He had spent his life in the so-called Christian Church, but had never been a Christian before, but a poor, deluded hypocrite, thinking that he was a Christian. A short time subsequent, he heard Andrew Johnson preach on sanctification. Got convicted for it, sought and found it, went home to his church shouting the victory and thinking they certainly would receive the good news with gladness, but how he was disappointed, when on his return, after a two weeks' meeting, he learned that they had held a church conference in his absence and turned him out, simply because he got Bible salvation, which we must all have or go down to Hell.

Dear Brother Dawson said to me, "Brother Godbey, I am no comeouter. I see the Church of God clearly revealed in the Bible and prefer to hold membership in it, but they have excommunicated me." So I took him into the Nazarene Church, and sent his membership to Dr. Brazee in Los Angeles, Cal.

(k) The only utility of the Church on earth is to get people ready for the Church triumphant in Heaven. In order to do this, every one must be born from above and sanctified wholly. The true Church on earth does that very work. The Church which is delinquent in that work is either fallen, and become "the synagogue of Satan," or, as in case of the Campbellite, not fallen because launched on Satan's bottom with nothing to fall from. Why do I use this plain phraseology? Because I have my eye on the Judg-

ment Bar, where I must meet all the people to whom
I have had a chance to tell the good news of salvation,
and to warn them against Satan's counterfeits, his
greased plank over which he slides deluded millions
into Hell.

The supernatural birth, i. e., the regeneration of
the Holy Ghost, is the bottom of the Christian experience we must all have if we go to Heaven. Campbellism is not only utterly destitute of spiritual regeneration, but I actually heard their preachers denounce
and ridicule it as wild fanaticism the first twenty years
of my life, making all manner of fun of it and doing
their best to prejudice the people against it so they
would think there was no such thing, and then would
come and join them.

Instead of preaching God's awful truth, "the soul
that sins, it shall die" (Ezek. 18:4-20), and getting
conviction on the people like a nightmare, so they
would see Hell open and demons racing from the pit
and reaching their fiery fingers after them to bind them
in clanking chains, and drag them down to spend an
eternity of woe in a burning Hell, till they would
crowd the altar and cry for mercy till the bending
Heavens would bring down showers of regenerating
grace and sanctifying power. they would spend their
time burlesquing Holy Ghost religion, till they would
preach away all the conviction the people had. Then
they would go to preaching "born of water" with all
their might, telling them that the regeneration is immersion in water, as Campbell in his *Christian Sys-
tem* positively states. Thus they run them into idolatry gross as the heathens, taking them to a mill-

pond instead of Jesus; thus making them idolators instead of Christians.

Suppose you are called a Christian when you are not one, you certainly know that the devil is as sure of you as though you were a drunkard or a murderer. To be called what you are not (with your own consent), is the very essence of hypocrisy, and most abominable in the sight of God.

(*l*) What about "born of water"? (John 3:5.) We want nothing but the truth, by which we will be judged in the Great Day. Will you not take the warning in time, before you stand before the Great White Throne? I tell you the plain and unvarnished truth, so I will be clear of your blood. You may reject it now, but you cannot, when the world is on fire. If you let Satan's preachers, themselves ignorant of God's regenerating grace and sanctifying power, hoax and delude you, you will be sorry when it is too late.

Nicodemus thought Jesus meant literal water applied to his body, *i. e.*, a physical birth, but Jesus not only corrected him in plain and unmistakable words, but castigated him for the awful mistake he had made, as he was a teacher in Israel and ought to have known better. You see, he thought, like the Campbellites, that Jesus meant a bodily birth, therefore he said, "How can a man be born when he is old? Can he the second time enter into his mother's womb and be born?" Jesus beautifully corrected him (v. 6), "That which is generated of the Spirit is spirit, but that which is generated of depravity, is depravity." V. 7, "Marvel not that I said unto thee, Ye must be born from above." V. 8, "The Spirit breathes on whom he will; thou hearest his voice, but canst not tell whence he cometh and whither he goeth; even so is every one who is born of the Spirit."

(m)   Jesus, in this wonderful sermon to Nicodemus, said not one word about the human body, nor a physical birth, but spoke all the time of spiritual things.   Religion is all spirituality, for which reason Campbellism is a random shot altogether, as it is destitute of spirituality, being infidelity on the Holy Ghost and idolatry on immersion.

That's the reason why it is so popular and takes so rapidly; it has no self-denial, but offers you a balloon ride to Heaven on flowery beds of ease, while others fight to win the prize and sail through bloody seas.   The way to Heaven is a death route, self-denial all the way, involving the actual crucifixion of the sin personality.   (Rom. 6:6.)

The preaching of Campbellites is simply an ingenious perversion of the Bible, which is a spiritual book, sealed to unspiritual people.   They give it all a mental or physical exegesis, thus missing humanity altogether, because the mind is not the man, neither is the body, but only his tenement, in which he abides during his probation.   The human spirit is the man, who possesses the mind and abides in the body.   This human spirit was killed by Satan in the fall, and that death has been transmitted by Adam to all his posterity, so that a spiritual corpse is the real status of every sinner.   You cannot commit a sin and retain spiritual life, as God says, "The soul that sinneth it shall die."   His Word is as immutable as His throne, and all true, whether we believe it or not.

In regeneration the Holy Spirit creates the divine life in the human spirit. "You hath he quickened who were dead in trespasses and in sins" (Eph. 2 : 1), Greek, *zooeepoiese,* from *zooee,* life, and *poyes,* to create. Hence you see the literal meaning is, He hath created life in you. Therefore, in regeneration the Holy Spirit creates the divine life in the human spirit, thus raising us from the dead. Without this resurrection, you are Satan's spiritual corpse, like the devil, the greatest corpse in the universe, and so you are fit only to abide with him in Hell.

When Jesus creates the divine life in you, by His omnipotent Agent, the Holy Ghost, He gives you the witness to the same, so you will know it better than you know anything else. We know what men have taught us, but when the Holy Ghost teaches you, as His work is perfect, you will know it indubitably.

Oh, how blessed this experimental certainty, which God has for His children, saving you gloriously from Satanic and human delusion, and humbuggery.

(*n*) In our Savior's sermon to the woman at Jacob's well, He mentions water seven times; whereas, to Nicodemus, only once. She naturally concluded that He meant the water sparkling ninety feet deep in Jacob's well, for which she had come a mile, as it was extraordinary.

He twice told her that she was mistaken, that He did not mean the water in the well, but the water of life, which He gives every truly penitent, believing soul. N. B. The Bible was never written with chapters and verses, those divisions having been made by the London printers, in 1551; who were so ignorant

of the meaning that their division frequently mars
the subject by breaking it in two in the middle.

Now wink at the fourth chapter division of St.
John's Gospel, and you run immediately into His
sermon to the woman at the well, in which He mentions the water seven times, she thinking He meant
the water in the well, but He correcting her twice
over, telling her He meant the living water which He
Himself doth give. He had clearly corrected Nicodemus, who thought He meant an operation performed
on his body; castigating him for his ignorance and
certifying that He meant a purely spiritual transac-
tion, with no allusion whatever to the human body.

The Bible reveals God Himself as the water of life
all the time. That life is symbolized by physical
water, but regeneration is God's own work and no
symbol. When the Holy Ghost regenerates you, He
creates the divine life in your dead soul; that life is
the water and He Himself the Spirit. Therefore,
"born of water and Spirit" simply means the recep-
tion of the divine life, created in your dead spirit by
the blessed Holy Spirit, and not a drop of literal
water in one million miles.

Alas, for the silly humbuggery played off on the
poor, ignorant people, by Campbellite preachers, Mor-
mon prophets, and Catholic priests, thus cheating them
out of the salvation which Jesus has for them and
which the Holy Spirit is on hand to administer!

What an awful ordeal awaits the false prophets
in the Judgment Day, when the people whom they
have deceived get their eyes open eternally too late,
and look them in the face and denounce them as

Satan's ministers, by him manipulated in the awful doom of damnation which awaits those who have gone through this world of Gospel privileges unsaved.

The people in the former dispensation used to cry out, "Prophesy unto us smooth things!" They are still at it. The popular preachers in all churches are prophesying smooth things, meanwhile the "Holiness cranks" are rejected and despised because they tell the truth. Rest assured, the day is very nigh when the tables will be turned and the despised "cranks," who have dared, fearlessly of men and devils, like Elijah, Elisha and John the Baptist, to tell the truth, the whole truth and nothing but the truth, will come to the front to abide forever.

(o) While Campbellism is radically deficient, and utterly bankrupt on the first great work of the Spirit, without which every soul is irretrievably lost in Hell, it is equally deficient on the second work of grace, which is absolutely necessary to keep us in the kingdom in the enjoyment of regeneration, and without which, none will ever be admitted into Heaven. (Heb. 12: 14.)

This theology is pelagianism, an awful heresy introduced into the fifth century by Pelagius, who taught that, when a child is born, God creates the soul and puts it in it, free from sin as Adam was before the fall. The Campbellites stoutly maintain that heresy, which I have had a chance to know, as I have had so many debates with their ablest men. See my autobiography and read my ten years war with the Campbellites. When He sanctified me forty-four years ago, making me a cyclone of fire, I was then in the vigor of my young manhood, flooded with the Holy Spirit and exceedingly hardy physically. Consequently I had great revivals everywhere, the Spirit falling on the people, putting on them a nightmare conviction, so that they would crowd the altar, pray through and get gloriously saved. Of course in my preaching I exposed the foolish and soul-destroying heresy of Campbellism without distinction or mercy. Consequently amid the multitudes that crowded my altars were many Campbellites who came like other sinners, prayed through and got gloriously saved.

My work so aroused them that an old debater sent me a challenge, which I utterly ignored and never answered. The work swept on in pentecostal power and he sent me another which I ignored, still the revival wave rolling on like a mighty sea and many Campbellites, as well as others, getting wonderfully saved, the audiences even through the week days as well as the nights, being paradoxically large and the interest wonderful.

One day a man pressing through the crowd notified me that Brother Corn was in the audience and wants me to preach on the conversion of Saul of Tarsus, and show the difference between the Methodists and Campbellites. This I did with great pleasure, showing up the fact clearly by the Lord's Word, that the Methodist has the experience taught in his doctrine and in the Bible, and if he keeps it, he is as sure of Heaven as if he were in it. Whereas if the Campbellite has no more than his doctrine gives him, he is as sure of Hell as if he were in it. Winding up with an invitation, the altar was again crowded with quite a number praying through and getting the victory, and among them a middle-aged woman, identified with the Campbellite Church, who shouted over the church, certifying that she had been deceived.

(p) In the conclusion, Brother Corn asked the privilege to speak, stating to the people that I was preaching error and he was willing to refute me if I would divide time and give him a chance. I turned the matter over to the people, who decided in the affirmative. Therefore the time and place were appointed. About two thousand people were present when we opened. I was unutterably suprised to find him so weak, as he was an experienced debater and had been very troublesome challenging the Holy Ghost preachers for a debate.

In my boyhood the Campbellites were exceedingly belligerent, claiming to be the only true people of God and challenging all others to meet them in debate; whereas the Methodist and Baptist preachers were generally afraid of them.

The next Conference made me presiding elder of my home distict, where I had been born and reared among them and they had done their best to drive Holy Ghost religion out of the country. When I' entered upon my district, I advertised in all the secular papers my acceptance of all the challenges they had ever made or ever would make. The result was a ten years war, which simply wound up because they had retreated from the field, giving up their belliger·ent policy, which had characterized them from the beginning, Alexander Campbell, their leader, having been a great debater. Consequently I have contested everything of their doctrine repeatedly on the controversial floor and found, to my sorrow, that they have no truth; but infidelity on the Holy Ghost and His mighty works, and idolatry on immersion.

(q) And they all this day make water essential to salvation and preach everyone to Hell who does not receive it. In my life-long study, with extraordinary opportunities, and my four tours in the Holy Land and the Bible lands generally, and reading the inspired original as readily and easily as you read the plainest English, I must candidly say, in view of the great Judgment, that, though at one time an immersionist myself, when I had no light on it, I find no solitary trace or track of it in the Bible. All those places where it speaks of going into the water and coming out, were inserted by King James' translators, who had been immersed three times, it being the current practice during the Dark Ages of one thousand years. At that time not one man in one thousand nor one woman in twenty thousand could read or write, and consequently they had water on the brain. There was little learning in the world three hundred years ago, and consequently they inserted those prepositions, which are not in the original.

For example, Philip and the eunuch, the strongest case in the Bible, I have actually seen the site of it eight times. It is simply a water-spout shooting out of the rock by the side of the road as you go down from Jerusalem to Gaza on the backbone of the mountain range between the Mediterranean and Dead Sea, only thirty to forty miles on either side; too short a

distance for a river, and no river is there, or immersion water of any kind nearer than the Jordan, seventy
miles away. This water-spout shoots out of the rock
and as it is excellent quality and scarce in that region,
they catch it all as it falls and no stream runs away.

(r) You remember when they called on Jesus and
Peter to pay their temple assessment and they had no
money, Jesus sent Peter to the sea to catch a fish
and get the money out of its mouth, which he did and
paid their assessment. Do you believe Peter waded
into the sea waist deep to catch that fish? You an-
swer an emphatic "No!" as no one but a fool would
have done it, and Peter was no fool. Why do we bring
up the case? Because the very same words are used
in reference to Philip and the eunuch going down to
the water and coming away. "Down" simply means
out of the chariot, antithetical to the "up" when he
went into it.

I have been at Jerusalem early in June, the very
time when the pentecostal revival took place, and if
I got a drink of water I had to buy it. It is a mountain city too high to dig wells, and it does not rain
there in the summer. Through the winter, the rainy
season, they catch all the water falling on their prem-
ises and store it away in tanks and cisterns beneath
their houses, but in the summer it gets so scarce it
is bought and sold.

(s) Here we have the case of three thousand in the
morning and five thousand in the afternoon coming to
Jesus and receiving baptism, as the symbol of the baptism which Jesus gave them that day with the Holy
Ghost and fire. There was no separate service for the

baptism and yet it was all over by the final benediction; with no immersion water nearer than the Jordan fifty miles away, and it was certain that they did not go to it.

They were all Jews who had been baptizing since the days of Moses, and as theirs was the ceremonial dispensation, in contradistinction to ours, the spiritual, they had one thousand times as much baptism as we do, receiving it every time they contracted ceremonial defilement; which they were liable to do whenever they went out in the city coming in contact with unclean animals, lepers, the dead, and Gentiles, so it was a common thing to receive baptism every time they came in from market.

(*t*) Every ceremonially clean person was competent to administer this baptism under the levitical law. Do you not see those women grouping together the converts, while the men, with their strong voices, were preaching to the multitudes on all sides, gathering them up and sprinkling upon them the water of purification, the only mode of baptism you can find in the Bible to save your life?

Here the commission in prophecy, as everything in our day and down to the end of time is in the prophecies: "I will sprinkle clean water upon you; from all your filthiness and all your idols will I cleanse you. A new heart will I give unto you, and a new spirit will I put within you and take away your stony heart, and give you a heart of flesh."

(*u*) I was reared amid predominant Campbellite influence, and they were constantly mocking and ridiculing sprinkling, so there was a prevailing and popular prejudice against it, looking upon it as unscriptural. All leaned to immersion, and myself among the balance, who constrained a Methodist preacher to immerse me in water, when under an awful conviction for sanctification and no Holiness people to tell me how to get it, and so many telling me that, if I would get immersed, I would have the victory, as the little sprinkle I had received in my infancy was not enough. Therefore I went for it, and received it in good faith, but, to my disappointment, found the change only from dry to wet, as old Adam, with whom I was having such an awful battle, like his snake and frog brothers, could live in the water as well as on dry land, and all my efforts to drown him proved a failure.

(v) I then sought sanctification nineteen years, preaching fifteen of those years. Meanwhile Satan was holding up the big baptism before me and tried to get me satisfied with it, telling me it was all I could get, till finally I lost sight of the water god and all other gods except Jesus, who then baptized me with the Holy Ghost and fire, giving me the victory, and the shout and leap have been getting better ever since.

There is actually no Scripture for immersion but those prepositions *into* and *out of*, which were not in the original, but were put in by King James' translators.

N. B. You cannot prove anything by prepositions and conjunctions, because they are no part of a language but only connections. Therefore we never use them in telegrams.

(w) What about the burial? It is all right if you let it stay where God put it, and let Jesus baptize

you with the Holy Ghost and fire, which crucifies the
old man of sin, called "old" because he is as old as
Satan. This is the baptism which has no meaning in
the Bible but purification, as Jesus Himself defines it
constantly by *catharidzo,* which has no meaning but
to purify. The "old man," *i. e.,* devil nature, is the
only impurity in the heart of fallen humanity.

When Jesus baptizes you with the Holy Ghost and
fire, He crucifies him, destroys his body and buries
it, not into water, but into His death, *i. e.,* the Atonement, *i. e.,* "the fountain filled with blood, drawn from
Emmanuel's veins, and sinners plunged beneath that
flood, lose all their guilty stains."

(*x*) If Jesus does not baptize you, Hell will ulti-
mately be your doom, as His baptism alone can crucify
the man of sin in every heart, destroy his body and
bring him into the Atonement, the sepulchre of all sin.

The sin personality that does not find an interment
in this magnitudinous sepulchre is sure to be buried
into Hell and drag its votary with it, to an eternally
deepening damnation. It is downright falsification
of God's precious Word and awful delusion of the
people, to put them off by burying their physical body
in water, to which there is no allusion whatever, and
besides by this diabolical perversion, they vitiate the
most important Scripture God has given them, reveal-
ing the baptism which Jesus came from Heaven, bled
and died to give every soul, without which there is no
hope.

(*y*) Mark 1:8; Luke 3:16; Acts 1:5; 11:16; and
Heb. 10:22. In these Scriptures we have the testimony of Jesus, John the Baptist, Peter, Paul, Mark,

Luke and Apollos, all certifying that the administrator handled the water and not the people. All the statuary corroborates it, which I saw again in the last year, having often seen it before, representing Jesus standing and John pouring the water on His head; and Paul standing and Ananias pouring water on his head. Besides, all the lexical authorities in the world certify that the New Testament baptisms were by affusion.

Origen, the first man in the world to write commentaries, in the third century, describing Elijah pouring water on the altar at Mt. Carmel (1 Kings, 18th chap.) uses the word *baptidzo*. The best dictionaries on both continents give "immerse" as a heathen meaning, and certify that it is never used in that sense in the New Testament. They corroborate their definition by allusion to all the cases. Such is the testimony of Schleus and Robinson and others.

(*z*) The paganistic origin of immersion is abundantly corroborated by the fact that the heathens all practise it this day. When, under Constantine, they poured into the Church by millions, unsaved, in the main, they brought in their heathen rites, as you see now in the Oriental churches which abound in idolatry.

The first great argument against immersion is that it is unknown in the Bible and was never heard of till after all the Apostles went to Heaven. The second is, it is very detrimental to spirituality, as it is so big you cannot take it without feeling it has something to do with your salvation, which is idolatry.

THE END.